75 QUILT PATTERNS

THE BEST OF
Helen's Hints

Helen Squire

American Quilter's Society

Located in Paducah, Kentucky, the American Quilter's Society (AQS) is dedicated to promoting the accomplishments of today's quilters. Through its publications and events, AQS strives to honor today's quiltmakers and their work and to inspire future creativity and innovation in quiltmaking.

Compiled by American Quilter's Society
Proofing: Hannah Alton
Graphic Design: Lynda Smith
Cover Design: Michael Buckingham

 American Quilter's Society

PO Box 3290
Paducah, KY 42002-3290
americanquilter.com

Additional copies of this book may be ordered from the American Quilter's Society, PO Box 3290, Paducah, KY 42002-3290, or online at shopAQS.com

Library of Congress Control Number:2019948661

Dedication

Dedicated to the American Quilter's Society members and *American Quilter* magazine readers who have supported "Helen's Hints: Creative Quilting Designs" for over twenty years.

Contents

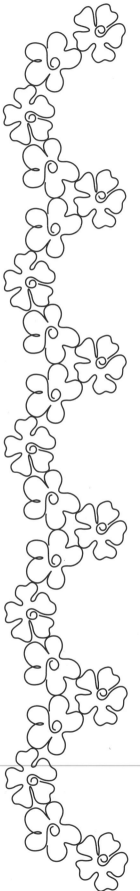

Contents

Introduction

Columnist Helen Squire is the well-known author of the "Dear Helen, Can You Tell Me?" series of quilting books, with over a thousand of her quilting patterns available in print form, as plastic stencils, and as computerized versions. For over twenty years, her column – "Helen's Hints: Creative Quilting Designs" – has appeared regularly in *American Quilter* magazine. Now, in honor of Celebrating 35 Years of AQS, she was asked to select some of her personal favorites and most popular patterns from previous *AQ* issues, to be known as "The Best of Helen's Hints."

Answering questions and offering advice come easily to Helen. Her career has encompassed a multitude of roles – author, lecturer, quilt shop owner, teacher, editor, and retired Vice-President of Sales & Marketing for AQS – but it was her education and her years in the fashion industry that were most influential to her career as designer of quilting patterns.

As you read her articles, you'll see that two words – "design", "pattern" – constantly appear. They're interchangeable, but they're not the same! In Helen's creative mind, "design" means an idea – a sketch – a motif. "Pattern" represents the final transferable form.

All 75 patterns are presented in their original size. Helen encourages her readers to feel free to make multiple copies of her designs for repeating patterns, increasing/decreasing her designs, planning layouts, and the mitering necessary for continuous quilting lines in their individual projects.

Quilting is an art form which has grown to meet the needs of modern quilters. It means many things to many people – a provider of items for comfort and/or necessity, an opportunity to gather socially to create, the joy of special gift-giving, recognition for services or contributions, cottage industries, and the joy of satisfaction and pride that comes from being able to say, "I made this for you."

Organizing Design Patterns Simplifies Selections

When you sort your patterns into categories, it becomes easier to find the perfect quilting design for your next project! Take a minute to think about what they represent to you. When looking back at the chapter headings I used in my "Dear Helen" series of quilting books, I took note of their groupings. Here are some suggestions or examples to get you started.

Subject: Sort by design subject, such as nature, flowers, marine, fantasy, holidays, children, or animals.

Style: Combine curves, geometrics, florals, scrolls, feathers, hearts, and so on into categories according to their predominant style.

Placement: Where will the design fit? Arrange according to different sizes of blocks, squares, triangles, borders, cables, or sashing; for instance, reducing or enlarging as needed.

Method: Divide the designs by the method of quilting they are most suited to – hand quilting, machine quilting, continuous lines, pantograph, etc.

Think about your needs and personal preferences. You probably use the same successful dozen or more designs you've always used. I know I do. Be adventurous! Analyze the shapes and purpose of your patterns, and keep in mind the fabric motif and the person receiving the quilt: masculine or feminine, age, hobbies, etc. Dig into your "stash" of newly organized patterns - and then let the quilting begin!

Placement Diagram

Four repeats with hearts facing out

Placement Diagram

Heartfelt 9"

One Quilting Pattern - Four Placement Choices

What can you do if you have only one quilting pattern but need to quilt a sashing strip, patchwork or appliquéd blocks, and alternate plain blocks? Well, just think about repositioning. Every pattern can be faced in, faced out, and repeated multiple times to create coordinated new designs. Heartfelt is a perfect example of how versatile a quilting pattern can become when you try different placement possibilities. Repeat the basic shape after enlarging or reducing to fit your project.

Heartfelt Sashing 2½"

Alternating repeats to form a continuous sashing or border strip

Heartfelt Heart 4"

Inward-facing hearts combined with a larger design motif

Multiple blocks with some design details omitted

Heartfelt Floral 4"

75 Quilting Patterns: The Best Of Helen's Hints

Yesterday's Treasures
Are Today's Designs

Modern Rosette
6½"

A recent display of 3,000-year-old rosette ceramic inlays from the palace of Pharaoh Ramses III at the Cleveland Museum of Art reminded me of Dresden Plate and Double Wedding Ring quilts. I realized they could be modernized into quilting patterns for today's quilters.

Placement diagram: This quilting pattern, shown set on point, connects to form a secondary design motif. Background fillers and grids would look great!

Petal Perfect
6½"

Adaptable Patterns:
Hand to Machine & Back

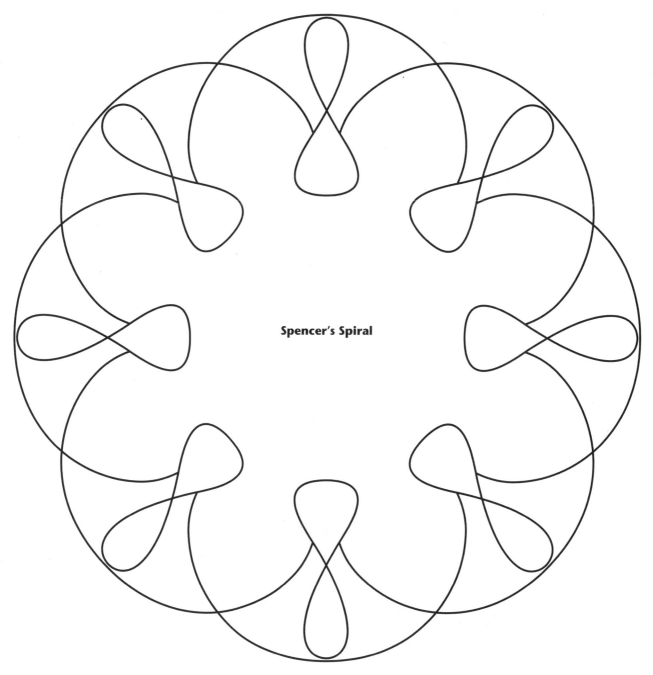

Spencer's Spiral

A newer twist on a Fleur de Lis design is used in Sara's Delight. The double row of stitches around the shape and center motif have been stripped down to the bare essentials, then simplified as demonstrated in the placement diagram for Sara's Delightful Border (page 13).

In Spencer's Spiral, some backstitching is required for continuous quilting, or the entire pattern can be quilted by hand as-is. The final choice is yours!

The nice thing about an open area is how it showcases and surrounds a pieced, embroidered, or appliquéd center or block.

Patterns can be enlarged
to any size.

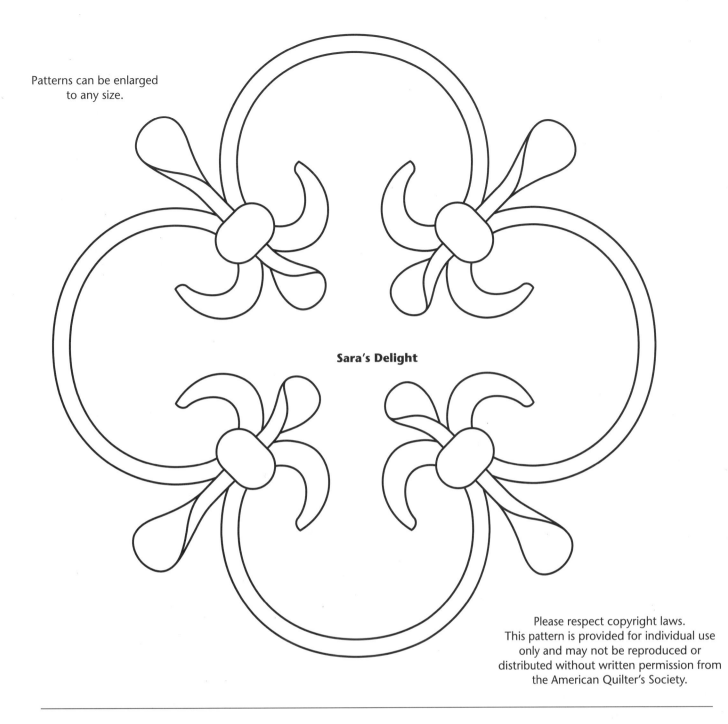

Sara's Delight

Sara's Delightful Border — Overlap multiple repeats, alternate details

Quilting Makes the Quilt!

**Radiance
Continuous 7"**

It has been said time and again—quilting makes the quilt! Never is that more true than with the addition of great quilting in award-winning show quilts. Superb stitches, overall placement, and appropriateness of the quilting pattern can be the difference between a blue ribbon and a red one.

Quilters who have mastered the art of quilting know the secrets of success: using a simple motif done right, repeating a variety of sizes, selecting a pattern that fits the area to be quilted and doesn't "float" in space, and adding texture to the surface with open, high-loft areas combined with flatter background

Radiant Flower 5″

Patterns can be
enlarged to any size.

fillers. The objective is to have a high-low effect that reflects lights and
showcases the overall pieced or appliquéd quilt.

To win in any quilt show, it is very important to enter the proper
category — quilted by hand, domestic sewing machine, or midarm to
longarm quilting machines; first quilt, group quilt, or mixed techniques.
Good luck!

**Norma Lee's
Ribbon Candy
2″**

Repurposing a Design Motif

As I was recently helping my friend downsize from a house to a senior apartment, we came upon some vintage doilies. There was one in particular that caught my eye—an embroidered cotton eyelet piece made in Austria a very long time ago.

Janice's Sashing 3"

Janice's Sashing 2"

Patterns can be enlarged or reduced to fit your project.

Janet's Design 7"

The potential for quilting patterns seemed limitless! Once a design motif is recognized or separated (see Janet's Design above), it can be used as the basis for an entirely new design and end use.

Since quilters never seem to have enough patterns that fit perfectly into sashing spaces between the blocks, I've designed some new ones for this purpose, Janice's 2" and 3" Sashing strips. Remember to enlarge or reduce as necessary. The width of the pattern needed will depend on whether the underneath seams are pressed to the sashing or to the blocks. It's important to avoid quilting through extra bulk.

My Heart Belongs to Baby

My Heart Belongs to Baby

This lovely baby quilt is made by combining ❶scrolls, ❷hearts, ❸cables, and ❹flower motifs. These design elements are connected with ❺diagonal gridlines that reverse along the sides, as well as a wide, offset ❻miter of the cable design, Jinny.

Jinny Variation

Muslin Master: Instead of sheets of paper, create a master pattern drawn on muslin
- Design and plan for one quarter of the layout.
- Flip, rotate, or reverse at center to fit size of quilt.
- Draw the quilting design on the muslin pattern with a fine-line indelible black marker.
- Pin light-colored quilt fabric on top of the muslin.
- Trace the entire design with a color-matched chalk pencil. Add batting and backing.
- Save the muslin master to use again and again.

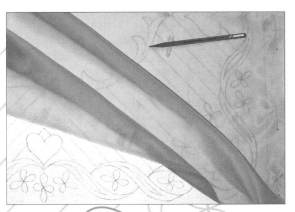

An underneath light source makes tracing easier.

Margaret's Baby Quilt

Pattern can be enlarged or reduced to any size.

Jinnys Variation
1½"

Jinny's Flower Bed

75 Quilting Patterns: The Best Of Helen's Hints

Can be enlarged or reduced to
any size to fit your project.

Brian's Baby Quilt

OUTLINE QUILTING
Outline, contour, or ripple rows of quilting can be used on double flowers, buds, leaves and stems.

CURVES & STRAIGHT LINES
Add visual appeal–anchor and minimize the fullness between the blocks by combining a box around a fancy quilting pattern. Adjust and alter the lines to fit the pieced area as needed.

Antique Rose of Sharon quilt top from the private collection of Helen Squire

Rose of Sharon: Traditional Applique, Non-traditional Quilting

There are several different variations of the Rose of Sharon appliqué pattern in *Carrie Hall Blocks: Over 800 Historical Patterns from the Collection of the Spencer Museum of Art, University of Kansas* by Bettina Havig (AQS Publishing, 1999), and at least a dozen versions appear in *The Collector's Dictionary of Quilt Names & Patterns* by Yvonne M. Khin (Acropolis Books Ltd, 1980). The quilt top pictured here seems to most closely resemble the Tudor Rose block in Mrs. Khin's book.

Books by quilt authorities Patsy and Myron Orlofsky and Ruth E. Finley indicate that Rose of Sharon was inspired by the Old Testament's Song of Solomon.

In the 1800s, Rose of Sharon became a favorite appliqué pattern and was often used as the "Bride's Quilt" made by young girls and quilted by their friends and relatives. These quilts were usually kept specifically for hope chests or

Mary Rose 4"

dowries. Most of them had heart-shaped quilting motifs, so superstition was that use of such a quilted gift before a wedding could result in a broken engagement or, alas, spinsterhood.

Outline, contour, or ripple rows of quilting can be used on flowers, buds, stems and leaves. "Double roses" with two layers of fabric are more difficult to quilt through by hand and make achieving a puffy effect difficult.

For a classic, old-fashioned look, take the time to preplan the quilting—but use today's tools and tips. Modern-day quilters can custom machine quilt around the appliqué or use a longarm quilting machine with an appropriate edge-to-edge heart-shaped pantograph pattern. A combination of techniques—hand quilting and machine quilting—is always a possibility.

Sharon
Border
2½"

Before You Quilt—
Important Things to Consider

POTTERY BOWL
Outline quilt around the bowl and then consider using a woven basket-like quilting pattern to add extra texture.

SASHING STRIPS
Pressed seams predetermine the size of the quilting pattern. Press seams either into the pink or toward the white block.

APPLIQUÉ SHAPES
Outline quilt around the birds, wing, bowl, leaves, and flowers. This lifts them up and gives them more importance.

FUDGE FACTOR
If a point is visually cut off when assembling the top, it is necessary to "quilt in" the missing tip, thereby completing the shape of the square.

BACKGROUND
When the color of the block touches the same color in the background, the area is quilted together, crossing over the seams.

PLAIN BLOCKS
Called the "Whipped Cream" part of the quilt, the seamless, wide-open area allows space to showcase a fancy quilting pattern.

Quilt top from the collection of Chris Moline

Yes, the type of batting and method of quilting—by hand or machine—are always considerations in the decision-making process of what and where to quilt. Equally important, though, is why certain areas have specific needs. For example: The blocks in this unquilted appliqué top are huge! They require careful planning: structural quilting; fancy quilting in the solid white half and quarter blocks; lots of quilting in the ditch; outline quilting around the appliquéd birds, flowers, and pottery bowls; and background fillers behind the blocks. Notice how the quiltmaker created an eye-pleasing design by combining straight sashing strips and rounded bowls—even going a step further by using a striped fabric for the bowls.

A Pair of Bluebirds

Embroider legs, beak, and eye details.

Continuing with the Bluebird theme, feathers would be an appropriate quilting motif in the plain blocks. Think big, full feathers in keeping with the scale and size of the blocks.

The concern here is the direction of the pressed seams in the sashing and intersecting squares. (For this article, the top was intentionally photographed over a darker fabric so the pressed seam allowances are more noticeable.) Seams determine the area to be quilted. Those pressed along both sides toward the middle require a smaller size of pattern than if both seams were pressed toward the block itself. You are restricted when some are pressed inward and some are pressed outward.

The Bluebird Border can be enlarged to fit any size of border, but it will be easier to quilt if there are no bulky seams under the bird's legs.

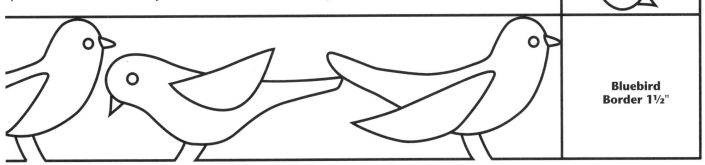

Bluebird Border 1½"

Bet You'll Like This Deal

I have a great deal of playing cards featuring art galleries, stately mansions, and beautiful places from around the world. I began purchasing them as inexpensive souvenirs while traveling. My collection has grown and turned into an interesting hobby, and I've certainly learned a lot about card designs! The traditional face-card imagery has been simplified here in King Henry and Queen Anne for easier quilting.

Placement Diagram

Card Trick pattern can be enlarged to fit your project.

75 Quilting Patterns: The Best Of Helen's Hints

Pips

King Henry

Queen Anne

Trivia question: Which card suit has the most value? Answer: In poker, it's hearts, diamonds, spades, and clubs in that order, and in bridge, it's spades, hearts, diamonds, and clubs. Quilt them along a patchwork border (in 52 squares) and you'll always have a winning hand!

A Modern Take on Quiltmaking

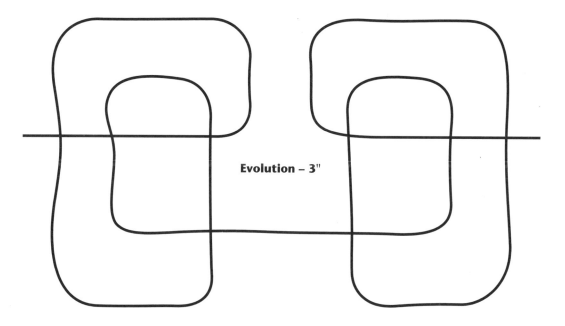

Evolution – 3"

Today's take on quiltmaking is simple straight lines where the fabric patches and colors dictate the quilt's overall design and where quilting plays a secondary and supportive role. Easier and simplified quilts that utilize quick techniques are in vogue. The one thing consistent with the past is workmanship! I've seen marvelous examples of beautiful quilts and quilting in this new modern category.

It reminds me of a Black & White Workshop where the intent was to use only grey-toned fabrics cut into rectangles. Quite a challenge! Besides needing a stash of black and white fabrics and light, medium, and dark grays, the various odd rectangle shapes themselves made fussy cutting impractical. Everything depended on creative placement and tonal balance. The quilting was considered secondary and mostly structural, done in the ditch. Not so today.

Quilting makes the quilt! Straight lines look better next to curved lines and curved lines look best next to straight lines. It is an old design principle used in Chinese porcelain and woven Turkish rugs. The eye is happier with the combination. My newest machine quilting pattern, Evolution, is designed to add softness and movement (combined with speed and adaptability) to your latest project. The straight-line bridge is perfect for connecting the stylized curves and is helpful when customizing or changing the size of a pieced block or borders in any quilt.

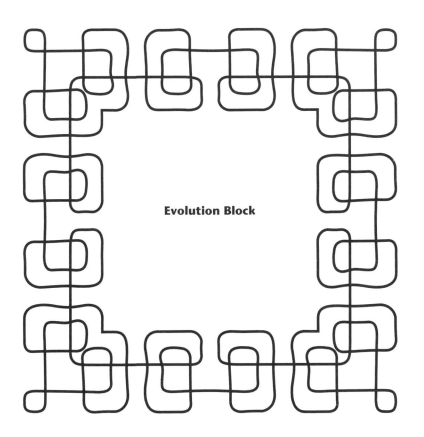

Evolution Block

Patterns can be enlarged, reduced, stretched, or shortened.

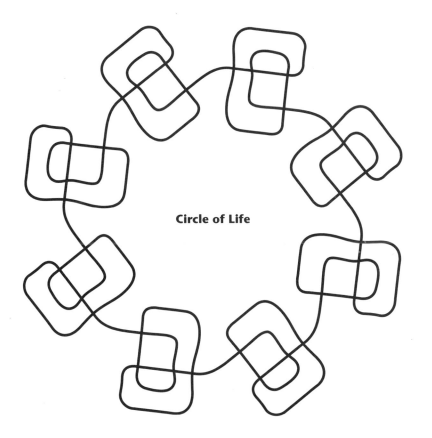

Circle of Life

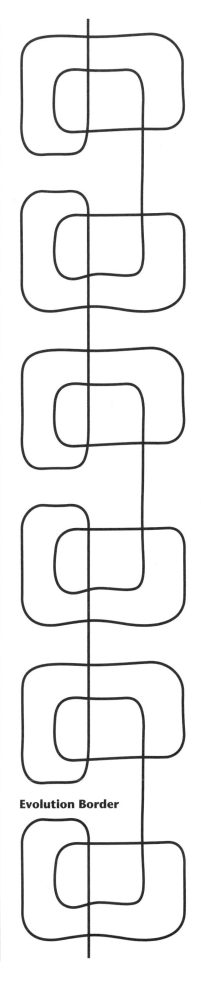

Evolution Border

The Origins of Quilting

When I was a young quilt designer in New York City, Averil Colby was my heroine. A well-known British historian, author, and quilter, Colby's research and insights into the origins of quilting became the basis for my interest in quilting. She concluded that diagonal stitching lines held fabric layers together longer and more firmly than lines following the straight woven thread. Certain patterns in quilting "made by the diagonal line, the spiral, and the scroll" have survived upwards of 2,000 years!

Modern meander quilting patterns need no marking, but other endless-type designs, such as my scrolling wave pattern, Averil, require the guidance of a template marked on the top layer. I prefer making a silhouette stencil template—one traced and cut from cardboard or a firm manila folder—to mark the circular outlines.

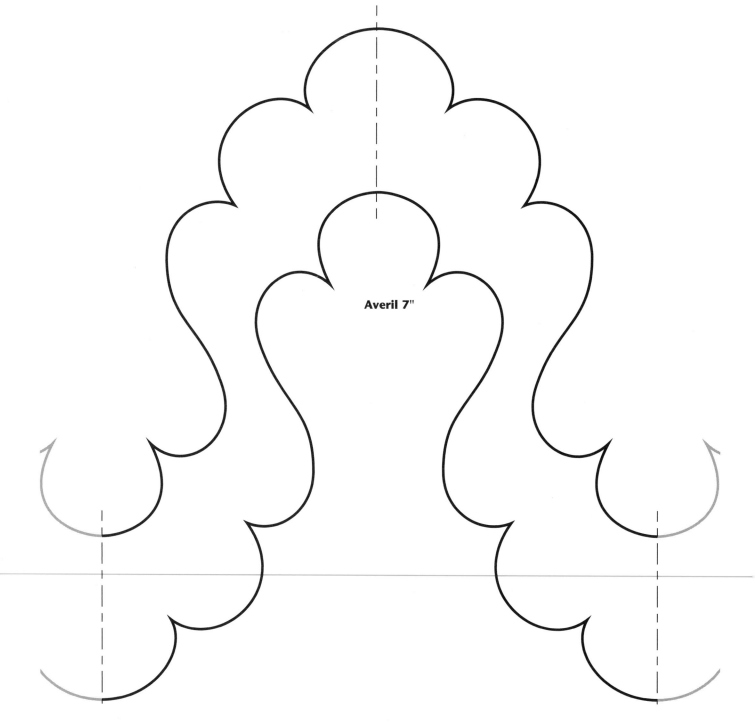

Averil 7"

Averil 4"

A silhouette stencil is easy to flip, overlap, and reposition on a quilt. Preplanning helps!

Placement Diagram

Quilted Hearts–A Timeless Tradition

Heart patterns have always been popular. As Mark Twain said, "There is no such thing as a new idea… We simply take a lot of old ideas and put them into a sort of mental kaleidoscope. We give them a turn and they make new and curious combinations." How right he was!

Above: Hearts & Diamonds is shown with lacy hearts on top and bottom and continuous repeats of the diamond rows.

Placement Diagram

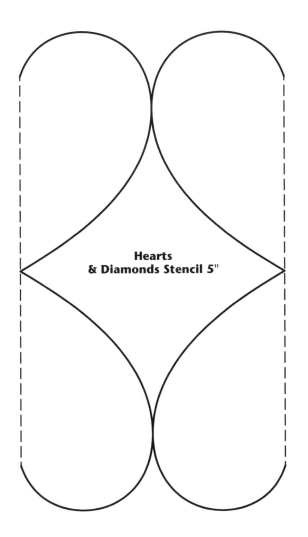

Hearts & Diamonds Stencil 5"

This two-part 5" silhouette stencil can be used to mark smaller borders. The diamonds really "pop" between the hearts when quilted.

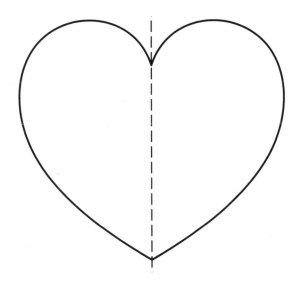

Hearts & Diamonds Border 3"

Sumertime Quilting

Summertime comes with picnics, parades, pinwheels, balmy breezes, warm sunshine, and plenty of time for daydreaming about your next quilt!

Whether it be a plain 4-sided or fancy 6-sided pinwheel, seeing them will usually make you smile and bring back a rush of fond memories. Consider using one of these designs when you need a quilting pattern for any playful quilt.

When alternating solid square patches with pieced or appliqué blocks, plan for the pinwheel size to be ½" to 1" from the

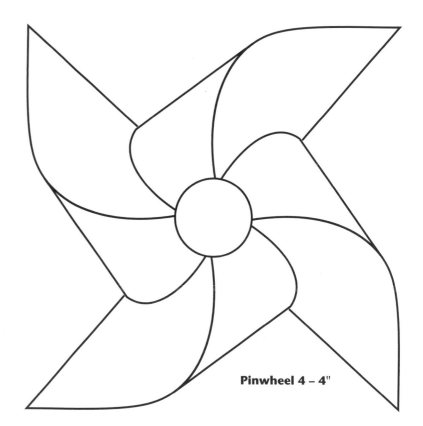

Pinwheel 4 – 4"

Enlarge patterns to any size.

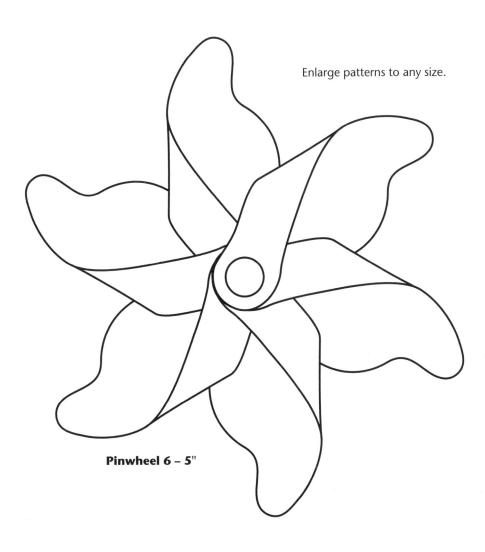

Pinwheel 6 – 5"

seams. This will prevent the quilting pattern from floating in space and the background from overwhelming the design shape. For a whimsical effect, try multiple repeats around/ along a border, but first mark them facing in the same direction—as if they were gently spinning in the wind.

Breezy Border 2"

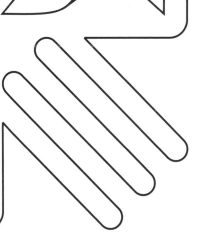

Garden Gate with Butterflies

Quarter-round quilting patterns are wonderful additions to any quilter's collection. These versatile designs become semicircles or full circles when aligned, rotated, and repeated. Garden Gate is no exception. It can be enlarged to fit any space and will fill the background, too.

And you never can have enough butterflies! There are four (4) different ones to choose from in Vanessa's Medley—incidentally, the word "Vanessa" is the name of a type of butterfly.

Quilting raises the outline shapes. Bright embroidered details and/or colored pencils would add sparkle and depth to the designs... and make them flutter like beautiful butterflies!

Garden Gate 7"

75 Quilting Patterns: The Best Of Helen's Hints

Garden Gate
Semicircle
Placement
Diagram

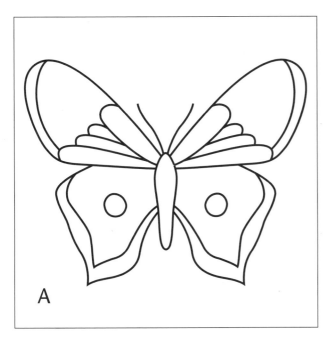

A

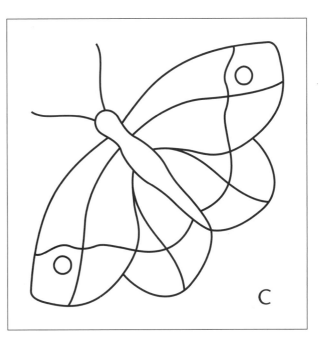

C

Vanessa's Medley

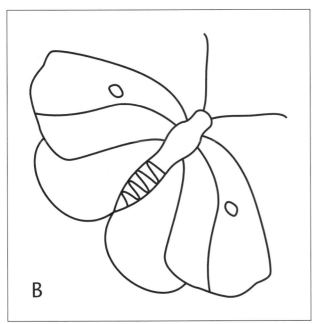

B

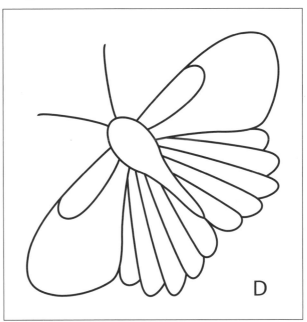

D

By the Sea, By the Sea...By the Beautiful Sea

As soon as I spotted this wave motif in a pebble mosaic along a pathway on the island of Rhodes, Greece, I knew the unique flowing lines were meant to be a quilting pattern.

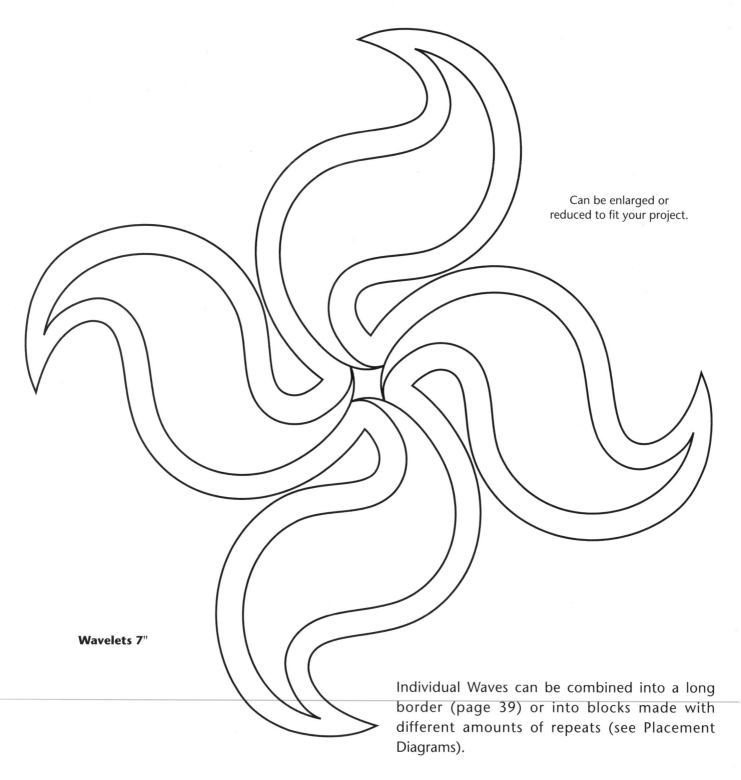

Can be enlarged or reduced to fit your project.

Wavelets 7"

Individual Waves can be combined into a long border (page 39) or into blocks made with different amounts of repeats (see Placement Diagrams).

In Wavelets, adding a row of Hawaiian-style contour quilting around the block seemed appropriate!

Placement Diagrams

Waves 4" x 9"

Sketches Today Can Become Tomorrow's Quilts!

As a fashion designer, I was trained to be observant and inspired by what I saw. As a quilter, I look for beautiful forms and unique combinations, something unusual yet useful. I'm forever sketching quilting patterns, no matter where I am, on restaurant napkins, backs of envelopes, or anything I can draw on. All I need is a small detail to remind me of my original enthusiasm when I saw something inspiring.

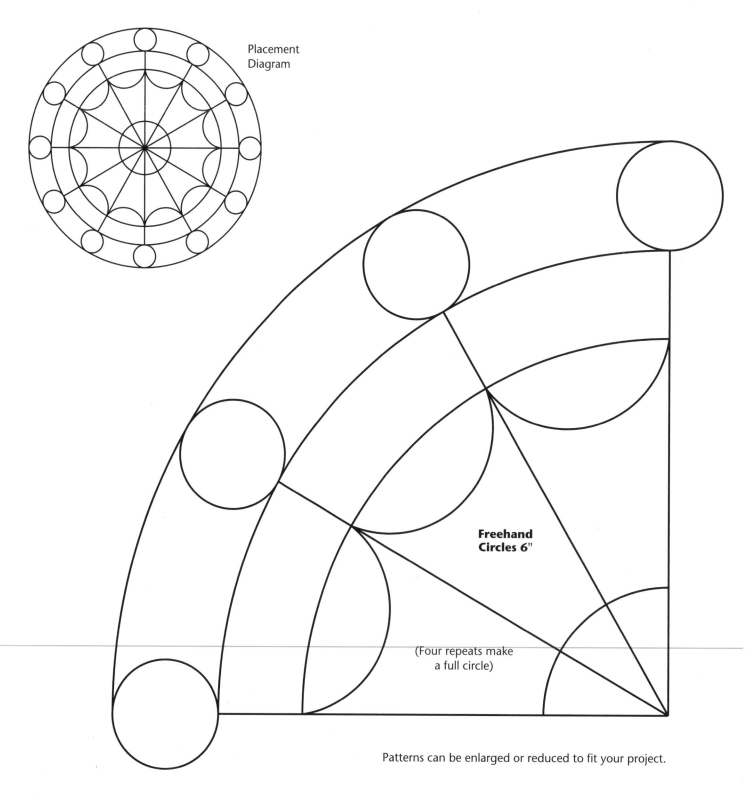

Placement Diagram

Freehand Circles 6"

(Four repeats make a full circle)

Patterns can be enlarged or reduced to fit your project.

Feathered Plumes 7"

While spring cleaning a few weeks ago, I found a file of sketches I'd made between March and August, 2009—my work files are labeled with location and date. This file turned out to be a treasure chest of ideas, and Freehand Circles and Feathered Plumes are two of them!

Most quilters today make instant digital records of exciting, eye-catching design details they like. A word to the wise—keep good track of them, because one day they may be just what you need for your next quilt!

Pentagon Flower Inspires Patterns

On Facebook I saw a photograph of a flower—*Tromotriche pedunculata*—and was instantly reminded of quilts! The purple and white colors, the perfect pentagons nestled within each flower, and most importantly, the fully-rounded dimensional shapes spoke to me. This is truly a flower that inspires quilting patterns!

Photo courtesy of Coleen Mannheimer

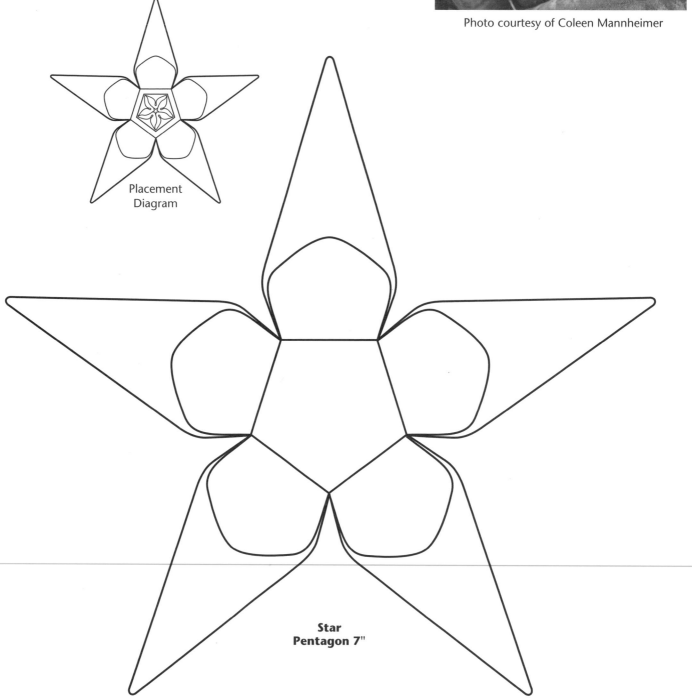

Placement
Diagram

**Star
Pentagon 7"**

However, inspiration is merely the starting point of a design. Experience, visualizing how the shape(s) will look after quilting, and the ability to modify the pattern for hand or machine quilting are important, too.

A quick search on Wikipedia provided information for Star Pentagons and Pentagrams (combinations) as well as "how-to" drafting directions. To keep with the five-sided theme, both of the patterns on this page are 5" in width. Feel free to enlarge or reduce them as necessary for your own projects.

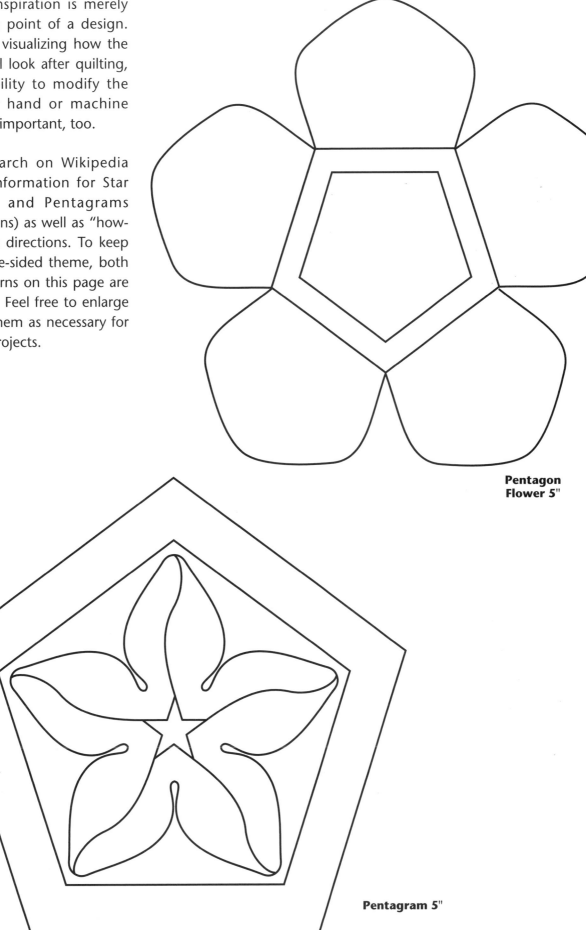

Pentagon Flower 5"

Pentagram 5"

Inspiration: Something Old, Something New

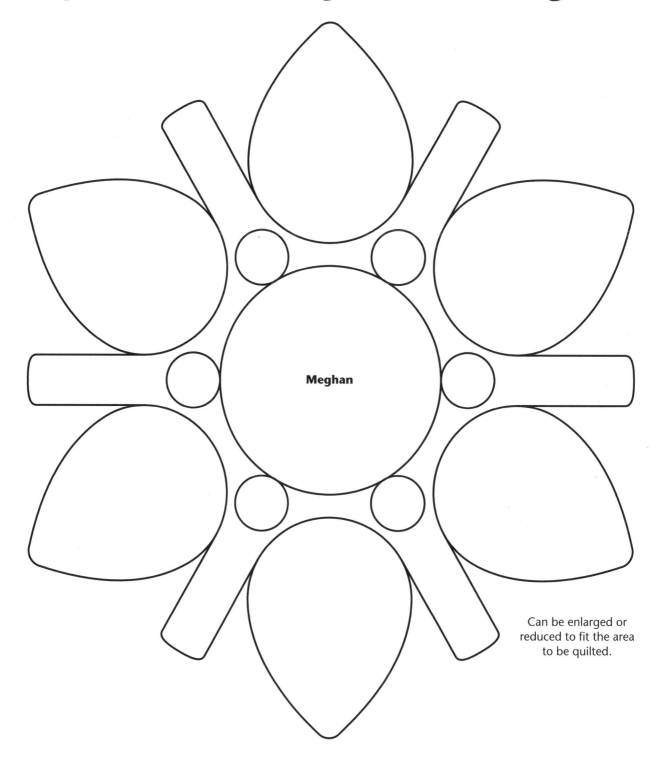

Meghan

Can be enlarged or reduced to fit the area to be quilted.

The world watched the fairytale May wedding of England's Prince Harry and America's Meghan Markle, who are now the Duke and Duchess of Sussex. I was no exception! Awed by the spectacular pageantry and outpouring of love, it was easy for me to find inspiration—for quilting! Two of my favorite royal wedding memories are the royal tiara Diamond Bandeau, entrusted to the bride for the occasion by Queen Elizabeth, and the 16-foot-long wedding veil embroidered with fabled English and American flowers. Incredibly, that's more than 5 yards of beautiful flowing fabric!

Placement
Diagram

In my pattern Meghan, I tried to capture the sparkle of diamonds and the elegant simplicity of the ceremony itself, and for Fancy, my goal was to create the lighthearted feeling of embroidery with curves, airy spaces, and soft edges.

Whenever you use a compact/dense inspiration—be it architecture, a flower garden, a brooch, anything—you have to consider how that detail will look when quilted. What is the basic essence of the design? Can it be recreated in cloth? What size should it be? The deciding questions for me are: Can I draw it? And if so, can I quilt it? Does it need to be adapted for continuous quilting? Is it accurate mathematically? And so on.

And the million-dollar question is, if I use this quilting pattern in a quilt, will it help me meet MY Prince Charming?

Fancy 9"

**Rose Marie's
Lace
7"**

Adapting Patterns to Continuous Line

When adapting designs from hand to machine quilting, keep in mind words like "simplify," "proportion," and "useful sizes." Always eliminate any extra details that could interrupt the stitching flow, and enlarge or reduce the original pattern to meet the size required for your quilting system. The scale of the design will depend on the fabrics used and the quilt top choices – large, medium, or small prints; flannels or plaids; geometric patchwork or floral appliqué; narrow sashing or wide borders; etc.

We all have old quilting pattern collections on paper or plastic. "Practice" is still the best word of all for changing them into designs we can use with today's newer methods of quilting.

75 Quilting Patterns: The Best Of Helen's Hints

Rose Marie

My pattern Rose Marie appeared in the first "Dear Helen" book—long before pantograph and edge-to-edge became buzzwords for quilters. It still looks good thirty years later.

Stacked

Placement Diagram

Staggered

Rose Marie Continuous 3"

Developing a Pattern Series

At a recent Sewing & Quilt Expo held in Chantilly, VA, I excitedly tried several of the standup quilting machines. This new design, D.C. Delight, was the result of my practicing freehand quilting. According to Sharon Schamber, an AQS author and award-winning quilter who was teaching there, my design incorporates basic elements of classic continuous quilting patterns—scroll, teardrop, scallop, and a soft S shape.

I traced the design from the quilted fabric onto a napkin and then made photocopies to play with later back in my studio. From the original motif, I developed a pantograph, double border, and corner variation.

D.C. Delight 5"

Potomac Pantograph

75 Quilting Patterns: The Best Of Helen's Hints

D.C. Corner

Chantilly Lace

Pattern can be
enlarged to any size.

**Floral Lei
Continuous 7"
Wreath**

Discovering Secondary Quilting Designs,

In quiltmaking we often use multiple repeats of the same pattern. By itself, Floral Lei is a lovely continuous double-line pattern, yet when four repeats are used (page 51), a secondary design is created by the open area formed at the intersection of the wreaths. Called negative space, it becomes an entirely new quilting design.

For a border or sashing strip, it's easy to adapt a pattern into a straight line. The real design challenge comes when creating multiple repeats for edge-to-edge quilting, as in Floral Lei Pantograph. I like to slightly nestle the motifs, thereby minimizing the open space formed between the rows.

75 Quilting Patterns: The Best Of Helen's Hints

There are two choices for this circular design: to position the main motif at 12, 3, 6 ,and 9 o'clock, or to position it at 2, 4, 8, and 10 o'clock. Choose the placement you like the best. Remember that the pattern that is set on-point will require—and cover—a larger area.

Floral Lei Pantograph

Pattern can be enlarged to any size.

Aloha 'oe, Ha'o wau ia 'oe (I love you, farewell, I miss you)

Ages ago, I designed a quilting pattern—Oval Flower Garden —with a crosshatched grid background. Each of its dainty flowers contained individual petals, perfect for traditional hand quilters (see above right). For today's machine quilters, I've designed something that looks entirely different—an energetic floral, quilted in continuous freeform lines that give the feeling of movement and emotion.

Patterns can be enlarged or reduced to fit your project.

Placement Diagram

The foundation arc I used is an elongated oval shape with two different flowers. Refer to the Placement Diagram (left) to produce a full oval made by reversing Vovo, then rotating 90°. In Aloha Scalloped Border (right), the shaded flower motif is overlapped to create a long connected chain.

The exotic flowers, especially those in the Aloha Scalloped Border, are reminiscent of the beautiful, perfumed flower leis of the Hawaiian Islands. They are a loving tribute to my sister, Florence Mae Andrade, who lived and loved in Hawaii for almost seven decades before recently passing away. Aloha, Flo—this one's for you.

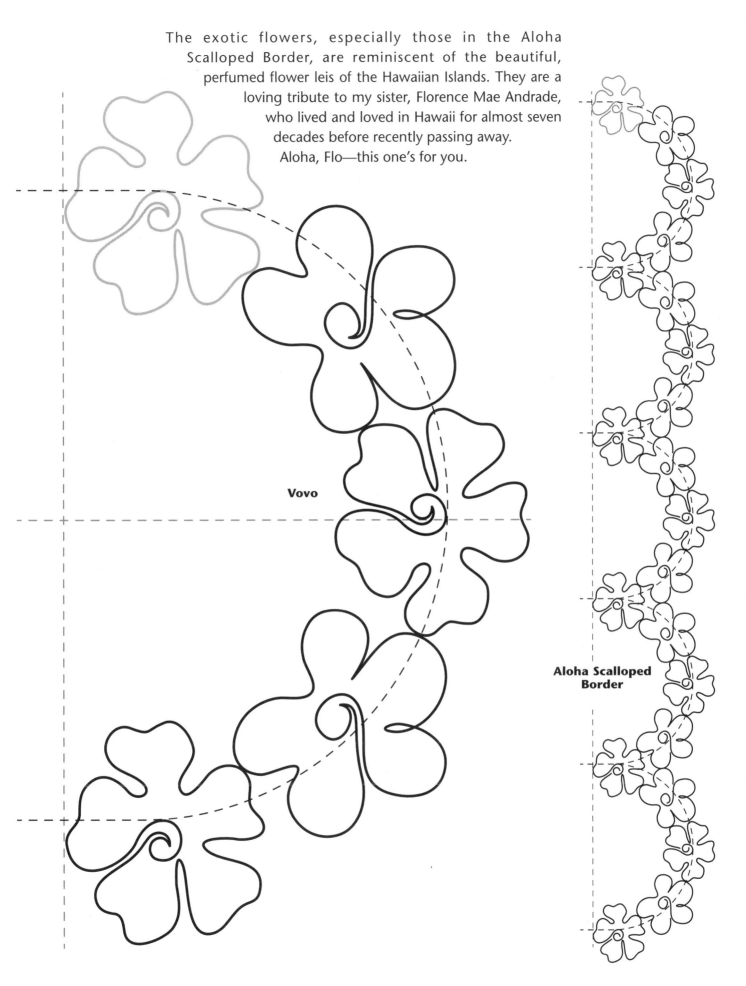

Vovo

Aloha Scalloped Border

Can be enlarged to any block
or medallion size.

Yoko's Flowers 7"

Marking Quilts with Silhouette Stencils

One of my first purchases as a quilter was a box full of old quilting patterns, all cut out of cardboard. Irregular, worn edges and overlapping pencil lines from countless markings surrounded well-used shapes of feathers, cables, and flower parts. Some motifs were almost unrecognizable until the silhouettes were retraced on cloth and finally quilted. A traditional way of marking in an earlier era was to cut popular quilting shapes out of wood in a variety of sizes.

Raindrops 2"

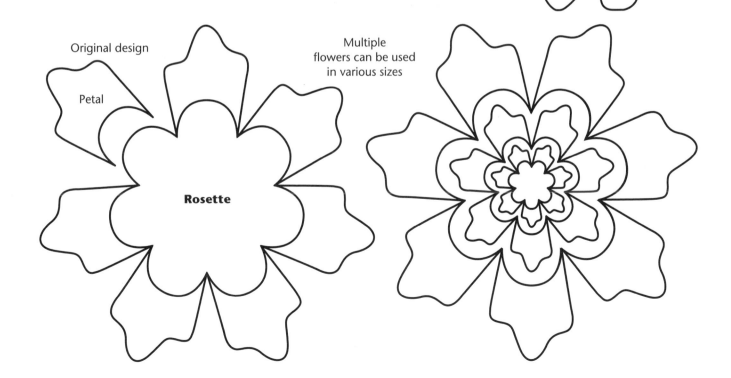

The best part of using a silhouette stencil to mark your quilt is that this method can be used before or after batting together the textile sandwich. I love to use it to darken the pattern shape if the original chalk line, preplanned and premarked, rubs off.

Enlarge the pattern to the desired size, then paste the page on to heavier card stock (a manila file folder is good). Cut out one repeat of the shape(s). Refer to the pattern placement as you trace around the silhouette to complete marking the design. For Yoko's Flowers, use a petal and the center rosette.

These simplified designs were inspired by my trip to Japan. There is an inherent beauty to the orderly repetition of each freeform shape, a serene sense of calmness.

Original design

Petal

Multiple flowers can be used in various sizes

Rosette

Winter Wonderland: Angel, Fairy & Snowflake

Remember when designs were printed on graph paper so that you could copy the shapes box-by-box? And how by changing the box size, you could enlarge or reduce the size of the pattern? Well, now you can do those same things by just hitting a computer key or a button on a copy machine!

Here are two of my favorite winter quilting patterns: Blue Ice Snowflake and Linda's Snow Fairy. Please feel free to change their size to fit your projects.

Little Angel Paper Doll is my gift to you for the holidays. Enjoy!

Little Angel Paper Doll

Placement Diagram

Linda's Snow Fairy

Placement Diagram: Gridlines drawn through Linda's Snow Fairy make it possible to redraw. Scanning or photocopying to change the size would be easier.

Blue Ice Snowflake

Quilted Presents From Santa!

Depending on where you live, Santa Claus might be known as Saint Nicholas, St. Nick, Father Christmas, Bishop Nicholas, Sinter Klaus, or even Knickerbocker Santa. No matter what you call him, you can be sure that this legendary bringer of gifts needs plenty of ribbons and bows for his universal presents. Here are a few quilted versions of them to use on your holiday gifts—and all year long, too!

Angel Wings and Ribbon Candy, on the opposite page, are block variations created by manipulating certain key elements from Gift Wrapped. Extra details were omitted, the corners were mitered, and a reversed copy was used to make a border. Refer to the Placement Diagram to mark in a continuous line, then finish it off with a bow of your choice!

As always, all of my patterns can be enlarged to fit your gift's size.

Reversed

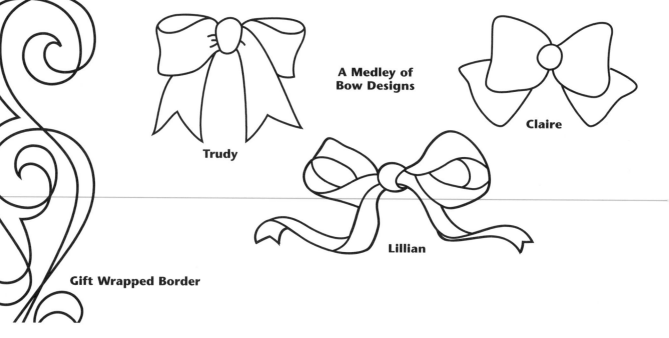

Trudy

A Medley of Bow Designs

Claire

Lillian

Gift Wrapped Border

Angel Wings

Patterns can be enlarged, reduced, stretched or shortened.

Ribbon Candy

Gift Wrapped

Adapting Patterns to Match the Quilt's Theme

Look very closely at these two completely different interpretations of the same basic border pattern. Both are easy to finger-trace into continuous line patterns for machine quilting. Holiday Braid has soft curved edges suitable for a decorative band-like edging. Military Chevron features lines or stripes in the shape of a "V". The placement is key—one faces up, and the other must face downward in order to be accurate.

These borders are not interchangeable. Instead, they are meant to convey a mood – feminine soft curves or strong straight lines that are more masculine in appearance. Both are sophisticated yet simple, and both add texture and dimension.

As a designer, I always give my quilting patterns a name for copyright reasons. But more importantly, the names should convey the flow of the lines as I draw. When the proper quilting pattern is selected, it should feel right and enhance the completed quilt and its end use—or user.

The width of these patterns can be reduced or enlarged and their length shortened or extended to fit any project size.

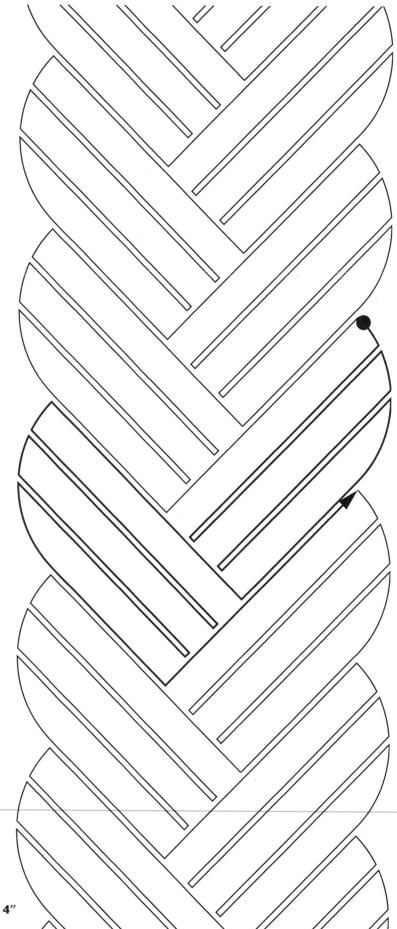

Holiday Braid 4″

**Military Chevron
4″**

Mini Designs
Add Extra Dimension
To Quilts

At the AQS QuiltWeek Contests, I noticed award-winning quilters were adding something new to their quilting. Smaller motifs of feathered plumes and scrolls were quilted into the background areas where intersecting filler patterns met, but you have to look very closely for these little gems hidden within the secondary design. I'm talking elaborate allover close quilting done on a quilting machine!

Background fillers are often used in a controlled, preplanned method to flatten areas between the pieced or appliquéd blocks and borders, and sometimes crystals are added for extra emphasis. Adding smaller design motifs in these spaces takes quilting to a whole new level!

Here are just a few of my published patterns that are absolutely perfect for this technique. Mini patterns—fluffy feathers, smooth swirls—combined with straight lines and traditional freehand fillers can add depth to your quilts, too.

**Dorothy's
Border Plume**

**Spun Sugar
Mini**

**Lily Pad
Swag Mini**

**Kaylee
Continuous
Medallion Mini**

**Penelope's
Plumes Mini**

This Mini Collection was
reduced 50% from the
original patterns.

Please reduce or enlarge them
as needed to fit your project.

Join the FUN!

Become a member of the American Quilter's Society, the largest membership-based quilting organization in the world.

$25